Easy Veal Cookbook

50 Delicious Veal Recipes

By
BookSumo Press
All rights reserved

Published by
http://www.booksumo.com

ENJOY THE RECIPES?
KEEP ON COOKING WITH 6 MORE FREE COOKBOOKS!

Click the link below and simply enter your email address to join the club and receive your 6 cookbooks.

http://booksumo.com/magnet

 https://www.instagram.com/booksumopress/

 https://www.facebook.com/booksumo/

LEGAL NOTES

All Rights Reserved. No Part Of This Book May Be Reproduced Or Transmitted In Any Form Or By Any Means. Photocopying, Posting Online, And / Or Digital Copying Is Strictly Prohibited Unless Written Permission Is Granted By The Book's Publishing Company. Limited Use Of The Book's Text Is Permitted For Use In Reviews Written For The Public.

Table of Contents

- 5 . . . . French Veal Stew
- 6 . . . . Spring Veal Stew
- 7 . . . . French Veal Stew
- 8 . . . . Roman Stuffed Veal Cutlets
- 9 . . . . Veal Cutlets
- 10 . . . . . . Emilia-Romagna Cannelloni
- 12 . . . . . . Tuesday's Lunch Burgers
- 13 . . . . . . Classic Swiss Veal Stew
- 14 . . . . . . Meatloaf Festival
- 15 . . . . . . Veal Marsala
- 16 . . . . . . Tuesday's Lunch Burgers
- 17 . . . . . . Veal Chops
- 18 . . . . . . Italian Style Veal
- 19 . . . . . . Countryside Veal Stew
- 20 . . . . . . Italian Style Veal
- 21 . . . . . . Veal Clásico
- 22 . . . . . . Stuffed Veal
- 23 . . . . . . Veal Wienerschnitzel
- 24 . . . . . . Veal Meatball Appetizer
- 25 . . . . . . Chicken and Veal Roast
- 26 . . . . . . April's Shower Bacon Soup
- 27 . . . . . . Veal Meatballs II
- 28 . . . . . . Veal Shanks: (Osso Buco)
- 29 . . . . . . French Sauce: (Demi-Glace)
- 31 . . . . . . Italian Style Veal Shanks
- 32 . . . . . . Easier Wiener Schnitzel
- 33 . . . . . . Sunday's Rustic Dinner
- 34 . . . . . . Tarragon Veal Steaks
- 35 . . . . . . Bavarian Style Veal
- 36 . . . . . . Milanese Veal Scaloppini
- 37 . . . . . . Tarragon Mushroom Entrée
- 38 . . . . . . Chops 101
- 39 . . . . . . Backroad Veal Stew
- 40 . . . . . . Homemade Scaloppini
- 41 . . . . . . Veal Fontina
- 42 . . . . . . Sicilian Style Veal Chops
- 43 . . . . . . Veal Escape
- 44 . . . . . . 25-Minute Veal Meal
- 45 . . . . . . Panhandle Cuisine Stew
- 46 . . . . . . Free City Veal
- 47 . . . . . . Simply Breaded Veal
- 48 . . . . . . Veal Parmigiana
- 49 . . . . . . Artisanal Veal
- 50 . . . . . . How to Make Rump Roast
- 52 . . . . . . Baked Veal Cutlets
- 53 . . . . . . Veal Shanks: (Osso Buco III)
- 54 . . . . . . January Night Veal Stew
- 55 . . . . . . Lover's Veal
- 56 . . . . . . Crepes and Veal
- 57 . . . . . . Mushrooms Sour Cream Stew

French Veal Stew

🥣 Prep Time: 15 mins
🕐 Total Time: 30 mins

Servings per Recipe: 6
Calories	261 kcal
Fat	10.5 g
Carbohydrates	19 g
Protein	18 g
Cholesterol	71 mg
Sodium	578 mg

Ingredients

- 1 1/2 lb. thin veal cutlets
- 1/4 C. all-purpose flour for coating
- 3 tbsp butter
- 1 tbsp minced garlic
- 1 tbsp minced shallot
- 1/2 lb. Crimini mushrooms, sliced
- 1/2 C. broth
- 1/2 C. veal stock
- 1 (10 oz.) can artichoke hearts, drained and sliced
- salt and pepper to taste

Directions

1. Lightly coat the veal cutlets with the flour and shake off the excess.
2. In a large skillet, melt the butter on medium-high heat and cook the cutlets for about 1-2 minutes per side.
3. Transfer the veal cutlets into a plate and keep aside.
4. In the same skillet, sauté the garlic and shallots till tender.
5. Stir in the mushrooms and cook till the mushrooms begin to sweat.
6. Add the broth and cook for about 2-3 minutes, stirring with a spoon to scrape the bottom of the pan.
7. Add the stock and simmer for about 5-10 minutes.
8. Add the cooked veal and artichokes and cook till heated completely.
9. Season with the salt and pepper.
10. In serving plates, place the veal cutlets top with the sauce.

SPRING
Veal Stew

🥣 Prep Time: 10 mins
🕐 Total Time: 1 hr 40 mins

Servings per Recipe: 4
Calories	464 kcal
Fat	25.4 g
Carbohydrates	6.9g
Protein	44.8 g
Cholesterol	204 mg
Sodium	512 mg

Ingredients

- 4 tbsp olive oil
- 1 onion, chopped
- 2 cloves garlic, minced
- 2 lb. veal, trimmed and cubed
- 1 (8 oz.) can tomato sauce
- 1/2 C. broth
- salt and pepper to taste

Directions

1. In a large pan, heat the oil on medium heat and sauté the onions and garlic till tender.
2. Add cubed veal and sear till browned evenly.
3. Stir in the tomato sauce, broth, salt and pepper and bring to a boil.
4. Reduce the heat to low and simmer, covered for about 1 1/2 hours.

Veal Cutlets

🥣 Prep Time: 30 mins
⏱ Total Time: 1 hr

Servings per Recipe: 6
Calories   673 kcal
Fat   43.3 g
Carbohydrates   25.4g
Protein   41.8 g
Cholesterol   190 mg
Sodium   1195 mg

Ingredients

- 2 lb. boneless veal medallions, pounded to 1/4 inch thickness
- 1 C. all-purpose flour
- 1 tsp salt
- 1/2 tsp ground white pepper
- 1/4 C. olive oil
- 1 lb. mozzarella cheese, shredded
- 1/2 C. vegetable broth
- 1/2 C. butter
- 3 tbsp all-purpose flour
- 3 tbsp fish broth
- salt and pepper to taste

Directions

1. Set your oven to 350 degrees F before doing anything else.
2. In a shallow dish, mix together 1 C. of the flour, salt and white pepper.
3. Coat the veal medallions with the flour mixture evenly and shake off the excess.
4. In a large skillet, heat the olive oil on medium-high heat and sear the veal medallions for about 1 minute per side.
5. Place the veal medallions in a 13x9-inch baking dish and sprinkle with the mozzarella cheese evenly.
6. In a clean skillet, melt the butter with 1/2 C. of the sherry on low heat.
7. In a small bowl, mix together 3 tbsp of the flour, 3 tbsp of the sherry.
8. Add the flour mixture in the skillet, beating continuously till thickened.
9. Season with the salt and pepper.
10. Place the sherry sauce over the veal and cheese evenly.
11. Cook in the oven for about 20-30 minutes.

ROMAN INSPIRED Stuffed Veal Cutlets

 Prep Time: 25 mins
Total Time: 1 hr 40 mins

Servings per Recipe: 4
Calories	772 kcal
Fat	42.1 g
Carbohydrates	43.1g
Protein	44 g
Cholesterol	177 mg
Sodium	1481 mg

Ingredients

- 8 (2 oz.) veal cutlets, pounded to 1/4 inch thickness
- 8 (1 oz.) slices provolone cheese
- 8 fresh asparagus spears
- 4 (1/2 oz.) slices turkey bacon
- 1 pinch salt and pepper
- 1 pinch garlic powder
- 1/2 C. all-purpose flour
- 1 egg, beaten
- 1/2 C. milk
- 1 C. seasoned dry bread crumbs
- 1/4 C. olive oil
- 2 C. sliced fresh mushrooms
- 1/2 C. chopped Vidalia onion
- 1/2 C. sliced roasted red peppers
- 1 C. broth
- 1 C. chicken broth

Directions

1. Season each veal cutlet with the salt, pepper and garlic powder.
2. Place 1 cheese slice over each veal cutlet, followed by 2 spears of asparagus, 1 bacon slice and another cheese.
3. Cover with a second cutlet, folding under and pressing the edges together to make a package.
4. In a plate, place the flour.
5. In a shallow bowl, add the egg and milk and beat well.
6. In another plate, place the bread crumbs.
7. Coat the veal packages in flour from both sides evenly.
8. Dip each one in the egg mixture, then coat with the bread crumbs evenly.
9. Arrange the veal packages onto a large plate and refrigerate for about 30 minutes.
10. Set your oven to 350 degrees F.
11. In a large cast-iron skillet, heat olive oil on medium-high heat and cook the veal packages for about 5 minutes per side.
12. Reduce the heat to medium.
13. Add the onion and red peppers and cook till translucent.
14. Add the broth, and simmer till all the liquid is absorbed.
15. Add the chicken broth and mushrooms and transfer the skillet in the oven.
16. Cook in the oven for about 30 minutes.

Swedish Veal Cutlets

Prep Time: 15 mins
Total Time: 45 mins

Servings per Recipe: 4
Calories   958 kcal
Fat   57 g
Carbohydrates   39 g
Protein   72.7 g
Cholesterol   306 mg
Sodium   1420 mg

Ingredients

- 2 tbsp butter
- 1/2 C. milk
- 1 lb. shredded Cheddar cheese
- 2 lb. veal cutlets
- 1 C. all-purpose flour for coating
- 1 tbsp butter
- 16 spears fresh asparagus
- 8 oz. crabmeat

Directions

1. For cheese sauce in a medium pan, melt 2 tbsp of the butter on medium-low heat.
2. Stir in the milk and cook till just bubbles begin to form at the edges.
3. Add the shredded cheese and beat till melted and smooth.
4. Remove from the heat and keep aside, covered to keep warm.
5. With a meat mallet, pound the veal thinly.
6. Coat the cutlets in flour, shaking off the excess.
7. In a large skillet, melt 2 tbsp of the butter on medium heat and cook the cutlets for about 1-2 minutes per side.
8. Transfer the cutlets in a plate and cover with a piece of foil to keep warm.
9. Trim the asparagus.
10. In a large pan of boiling water, blanch the asparagus for about 2 minutes.
11. In microwave, heat the cooked crab meat.
12. In serving plates, place the veal cutlets and top with the crab meat, followed by asparagus.
13. Serve with a topping of the cheese sauce.

EMILIA-ROMAGNA
Cannelloni

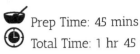

Prep Time: 45 mins
Total Time: 1 hr 45 mins

Servings per Recipe: 8
Calories	557 kcal
Fat	30.1 g
Carbohydrates	39.3g
Protein	32.5 g
Cholesterol	145 mg
Sodium	1423 mg

Ingredients

CREPES
2 eggs
2/3 C. milk
1 tbsp butter, melted
1/2 C. all-purpose flour
1/4 tsp salt
MEAT FILLING
1/4 lb. ground veal
1/4 lb. ground chicken
1/2 lb. ground beef
2 tbsp butter
1 tbsp minced fresh parsley
1/2 C. grated Parmesan cheese
1/2 tsp salt

1 dash ground black pepper
1 dash ground nutmeg
WHITE SAUCE
2 tbsp butter
2 tbsp all-purpose flour
1 C. milk
1/4 tsp salt
1/8 tsp ground black pepper
1/8 tsp ground nutmeg
1 (32 oz.) jar tomato pasta sauce
1 (16 oz.) package shredded mozzarella cheese
1/4 C. grated Parmesan cheese

Directions

1. For crepes in a bowl, add the eggs and beat well.
2. Add the milk, butter and beat well.
3. Add the flour and salt and beat till smooth. (Mixture will be best if left to set for about 1/2 hour before using).
4. Heat a medium skillet and cook 6-8-inch crepes till browned completely.
5. Set your oven to 375 degrees F.
6. For meat filling in a large skillet, melt the butter on medium-high heat and sear the veal, chicken and beef till browned completely.
7. Stir in the parsley, cheese, salt, pepper and nutmeg.
8. Remove from the heat and keep aside to cool.

9. Meanwhile for white sauce in a small pan over medium heat, cook the flour and butter for about 1 minute.
10. Stir in the salt, pepper and nutmeg.
11. Stir in the milk and cook, stirring continuously till the sauce becomes thick.
12. In the bottom of a 13x9-inch baking dish, spread 1/2 of the pasta sauce evenly. In the bottom of a 9x13 inch baking dish.
13. Fill the prepared crepes with the meat mixture, folding over all sides of crepe to form palm-sized bundles.
14. Place filled crepes, seam side down in the baking dish.
15. Spread the remaining pasta sauce over the crepes, followed by white sauce, mozzarella cheese and Parmesan cheese evenly.
16. Cook in the oven for about 20-30 minutes.
17. Serve hot.

TUESDAY'S
Lunch Burgers

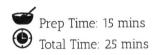
Prep Time: 15 mins
Total Time: 25 mins

Servings per Recipe: 4
Calories 352 kcal
Fat 14.8 g
Carbohydrates 26.8 g
Protein 26.5 g
Cholesterol 126 mg
Sodium 555 mg

Ingredients

1 slice bread, torn into small pieces
2 tbsp milk
1 tbsp Worcestershire sauce
1 egg
2 basil leaves, chopped
1 tsp minced fresh rosemary
1 tsp pepper
1 lb. ground veal
4 (1 oz.) slices Cheddar cheese (optional)
4 hamburger buns

Directions

1. Set your grill for medium heat and lightly, grease the grill grate.
2. In a bowl, place the torn bread and drizzle with the milk and Worcestershire sauce.
3. Add the egg and mix till combined.
4. Add the veal, basil, rosemary and pepper and mix till well combined.
5. Make 4 equal sized patties from the mixture.
6. Cook the veal burgers on the grill for about 5 minutes from both sides.
7. Place a slice of cheese on each burger and let it melt for about 1 minute before serving over the buns.

Classic Swiss Veal Stew

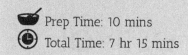

Prep Time: 10 mins
Total Time: 7 hr 15 mins

Servings per Recipe: 4
Calories　　　　　651 kcal
Fat　　　　　　　21.4 g
Carbohydrates　　59.9 g
Protein　　　　　53.1 g
Cholesterol　　　228 mg
Sodium　　　　　1003 mg

Ingredients

1 3/4 C. Swanson(R) Chicken Stock
1 (10.75 oz.) can Campbell's(R) Condensed Cream of Potato Soup
1 tsp dried thyme leaves, crushed
1 1/2 lb. veal for stew
1 (8 oz.) package sliced mushrooms
8 green onions, sliced
2 tbsp all-purpose flour
1/4 C. water
1 C. shredded Swiss cheese
Hot cooked egg noodles
Freshly ground black pepper

Directions

1. In a 3 1/2-quart slow cooker, mix together the stock, soup, thyme, veal, mushrooms and green onions.
2. Set the slow cooker on Low and cook, covered for about 7-8 hours.
3. In a small bowl, add the flour and water and mix till smooth.
4. Add the flour mixture in the slow cooker and stir to combine.
5. Now, set the slow cooker on High and cook, covered for about 5 minutes.
6. Stir in the cheese and black pepper.
7. Serve over the noodles.

MEATLOAF
Festival

 Prep Time: 15 mins
Total Time: 1 hr 15 mins

Servings per Recipe: 8
Calories   236 kcal
Fat   7.4 g
Carbohydrates   19.6g
Protein   22.7 g
Cholesterol   104 mg
Sodium   921 mg

Ingredients

2 lb. ground veal
1 C. Italian seasoned bread crumbs
1 egg, beaten
1/3 C. shredded baby carrots
1 C. ketchup
1 tbsp chopped garlic
1/2 C. chopped onion
1 tsp salt
1 tsp dried parsley
1/2 tsp chili powder
1/2 tsp ground black pepper

Directions

1. Set your oven to 375 degrees F before doing anything else.
2. In a bowl, add the veal, bread crumbs, egg, baby carrots, 1/2 C. of the ketchup, garlic, onion, salt, parsley, chili powder and pepper and mix till well combined.
3. Place the mixture into an 8x8-inch baking dish and shape into a loaf.
4. Spread the remaining ketchup on top evenly.
5. Cover the baking dish and cook in the oven for about 45 minutes.
6. Uncover, and cook in the oven for about 15 minutes.
7. Remove from the oven and keep aside for about 10 minutes before serving.

Veal Marsala

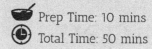
Prep Time: 10 mins
Total Time: 50 mins

Servings per Recipe: 2
Calories   504 kcal
Fat   22.8 g
Carbohydrates   27.4g
Protein   29.8 g
Cholesterol   135 mg
Sodium   225 mg

Ingredients

- 1/3 C. all-purpose flour
- 1 lb. veal cutlets, pounded thin
- 1 tbsp olive oil
- 1 tbsp butter
- 1/2 C. seeded and chopped tomato
- 1/2 C. broth
- 2 tbsp grated Parmesan cheese
- 2 tbsp chopped fresh basil
- 2 cloves garlic, crushed

Directions

1. Set your oven to 325 degrees F before doing anything else.
2. In a shallow dish, place the flour.
3. Coat the veal cutlets into flour evenly, shaking off the excess.
4. In a large skillet, heat the olive oil and butter on medium heat and sear the veal in batches for about 3-5 minutes per side.
5. Transfer the veal cutlets into a large baking dish.
6. Place the tomatoes and broth over the veal cutlets and sprinkle with the Parmesan cheese, basil, and garlic.
7. Cook in the oven for about 30 minutes.

GARDEN PARTY
Burgers

🥣 Prep Time: 20 mins
🕐 Total Time: 1 hr 10 mins

Servings per Recipe: 4
Calories   238 kcal
Fat   7.4 g
Carbohydrates   23.2g
Protein   18.4 g
Cholesterol   104 mg
Sodium   286 mg

Ingredients

1 lb. ground veal
4 crusty bread rolls, split
1/4 C. lightly packed chopped fresh basil
1 egg
2 tbsp Maille(R) Old Style Mustard, divided
1/2 tsp black pepper
1 medium red bell pepper, quartered

Directions

1. Set your grill for medium heat and lightly, grease the grill grate.
2. Remove some bread from cut sides of top half of rolls, creating a pocket.
3. In a food processor, add removed bread and pulse till fine crumbs form.
4. Reserve 1/4 C. of the crumbs for burgers.
5. In a large bowl, add the ground veal, bread crumbs, basil, egg, 1 Tbsp mustard and black pepper and mix till well combined.
6. Make 4 (1/2-inch) thick patties from the mixture.
7. Arrange the patties and bell pepper onto prepared grill grate over ash-covered coals.
8. Cook the peppers on the grill for about 7-11 minutes, flipping occasionally.
9. Cook the peppers on the grill for about 10-12 minutes, flipping occasionally.
10. Spread remaining 1 tbsp of the mustard on bottom half of the rolls.
11. Place rolls, cut sides down on grill grate and cook till lightly toasted.
12. Cut pepper quarters in half lengthwise and arrange on roll bottoms.
13. Top with the burgers.
14. Close the sandwiches.

Veal Chop with Portobello Mushrooms

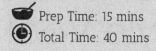

Prep Time: 15 mins
Total Time: 40 mins

Servings per Recipe: 2	
Calories	555 kcal
Fat	45.2 g
Carbohydrates	5.2g
Protein	21.7 g
Cholesterol	97 mg
Sodium	838 mg

Ingredients

5 tbsp olive oil, divided
1 tbsp butter
2 veal chops
1 Portobello mushroom, sliced
1 1/2 C. chicken broth
1 1/2 tsp fresh rosemary, chopped
1/2 C. broth

Directions

1. In a skillet, heat 4 tbsp of the olive oil and butter on medium-high heat and sear the chops for about 2-3 minutes per side.
2. Stir in the mushrooms and cook for about 1 minute.
3. Add the chicken broth and rosemary and simmer, covered for about 10 minutes.
4. Stir in the broth and increase the heat.
5. Cook, uncovered till the sauce reduces by half.
6. Veal chops may be removed at any time to prevent over-cooking, then returned to the pan for the final minute.
7. Serve with a drizzling of the remaining olive oil.

ITALIAN
Style Veal

🥣 Prep Time: 15 mins
🕐 Total Time: 40 mins

Servings per Recipe: 4
Calories 364 kcal
Fat 15.7 g
Carbohydrates 32.5g
Protein 23.3 g
Cholesterol 121 mg
Sodium 468 mg

Ingredients

1 egg
1 tbsp lemon juice
1 tbsp milk
1/2 C. all-purpose flour
1/2 C. Italian seasoned bread crumbs
1/2 C. grated pecorino Romano cheese
1/2 tsp adobo seasoning
1 tsp olive oil
4 (4 oz.) thinly-sliced veal cutlets
1 1/2 C. arugula, divided
4 tbsp golden raisins, divided
4 tsp balsamic vinegar, divided
4 tsp olive oil, divided

Directions

1. Set your oven to 350 degrees F before doing anything else.
2. In a shallow bowl, add the flour.
3. In a second shallow bowl, add the egg, lemon juice and milk and beat well.
4. In a third shallow bowl, mix together the Italian crumbs, pecorino Romano cheese and adobo seasoning.
5. Coat each veal cutlet in flour evenly.
6. Now, dip in egg mixture and coat into bread crumb mixture evenly.
7. In a skillet, heat 1 tsp of the olive oil on medium heat and stir fry the veal cutlets for about 1 minute per side.
8. Transfer veal cutlets into a baking dish.
9. Cook in the oven for about 20-25 minutes.
10. Transfer the veal cutlets into 4 serving plates and top each cutlet with 1/4 of the arugula, followed by the raisins.
11. Serve with a drizzling of 1 tsp of the balsamic vinegar and 1 tsp of the olive oil over each plate.

Countryside Veal Stew

Prep Time: 1 hr
Total Time: 2 hr 30 mins

Servings per Recipe: 8
Calories	414 kcal
Fat	13.3 g
Carbohydrates	23g
Protein	48.9 g
Cholesterol	255 mg
Sodium	284 mg

Ingredients

- 4 lb. veal shoulder roast
- 1/4 tsp dried thyme
- 4 carrots, halved
- 1 lb. small potatoes
- 1/2 lb. small white onions
- 1/2 lb. mushrooms
- 2 tbsp all-purpose flour
- 1 (10 oz.) package frozen green peas
- 2 egg yolks

Directions

1. Heat a large Dutch oven on medium-high heat and sear the roast till browned from all sides.
2. Add thyme and 2 C. of the water and bring to a boil.
3. Reduce the heat to low and simmer, covered for about 30 minutes.
4. Add the carrots, potatoes and onions and simmer, covered for about 30 minutes.
5. Stir in the mushrooms and simmer, covered for about 15 minutes.
6. With a slotted spoon, transfer the roast and vegetables into a large bowl and keep warm.
7. In a small bowl, dissolve the flour in 2 tbsp of the water.
8. Slowly, add the flour mixture into Dutch oven and stir to combine.
9. Cook, stirring continuously till the gravy becomes slightly thick.
10. Stir in the peas and cook till heated completely.
11. In a small bowl, add the egg yolks and beat and then stir in a small amount of the hot gravy.
12. Slowly pour egg yolk mixture into the gravy, beating continuously till thickened.
13. Place some gravy over the veal and vegetables and serve alongside the remaining gravy in a gravy boat.

MEDITERRANEAN
Moussaka

 Prep Time: 30 mins
Total Time: 1 hr 15 mins

Servings per Recipe: 6
Calories   408 kcal
Fat   27.4 g
Carbohydrates   21.4g
Protein   21 g
Cholesterol   130 mg
Sodium   476 mg

Ingredients

2 medium eggplant, thinly sliced
1/4 C. vegetable oil
2 tbsp butter
1 large onion, chopped
1 clove garlic, chopped
1 lb. ground veal
salt and pepper to taste
1 tbsp tomato paste
2 tbsp chopped fresh parsley
1/2 C. beef stock
1/4 C. bread crumbs
2 tbsp all-purpose flour
2 tbsp butter
1 egg yolk, beaten
1 C. milk
1/2 C. feta cheese

Directions

1. Set the broiler of your oven and grease a 9-inch square baking dish
2. Coat the eggplant slices with the oil and arrange on a baking sheet.
3. Cook under the broiler for about 5 minutes.
4. Now, set the oven to 350 degrees F.
5. In a large skillet, melt 2 tbsp of the butter on medium heat.
6. Add the onions and garlic and sauté till softened.
7. Crumble in the veal and cook until evenly browned.
8. Reduce the heat to low.
9. Stir in the tomato paste, parsley, beef stock, salt and pepper and simmer for about 15 minutes.
10. Stir in the bread crumbs, reserving 1 tbsp for later.
11. Remove from the heat and keep aside.
12. In a small pan, melt the remaining butter on medium heat and stir in the flour till smooth.
13. Slowly stir in the milk till no lumps form.
14. Simmer, stirring continuously till thickened.
15. Remove from the heat and add the egg yolk, beating continuously.
16. In the bottom of the prepared baking dish, place a layer of eggplant, followed by half of the veal mixture and half of the feta cheese.
17. Repeat the layers and then place remaining eggplant in a layer on top.
18. Place the sauce on top and sprinkle with the reserved bread crumbs.
19. Cook in the oven for about 45 minutes.

Veal Clásico

Prep Time: 30 mins
Total Time: 30 mins

Servings per Recipe: 4
Calories	301 kcal
Fat	14.4 g
Carbohydrates	11g
Protein	21 g
Cholesterol	82 mg
Sodium	131 mg

Ingredients

- 4 boneless, skinless veal cutlets
- 2 tbsp flour
- 4 tbsp butter, divided
- 2 C. mushrooms, sliced
- 3/4 C. broth
- 1/4 C. water (optional)
- 2 tbsp fresh parsley, chopped
- 1/4 tsp rosemary (optional)

Directions

1. Pound the veal till thin.
2. Coat the veal with flour lightly from both sides.
3. In large skillet, melt 2 tbsp of the butter on medium heat and sauté the mushrooms for about 10 minutes.
4. Transfer the mushrooms in a plate and keep aside.
5. In the same skillet, melt the remaining 2 tbsp of the butter and cook the veal for about 4 minutes per side.
6. Transfer the veal into a serving platter.
7. In the skillet, add mushrooms, broth, water, parsley and rosemary and cook till heated completely.
8. Place the mushroom mixture over the veal and serve.

STUFFED Veal

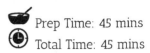

Prep Time: 45 mins
Total Time: 45 mins

Servings per Recipe: 15
Calories	261 kcal
Fat	11.7 g
Carbohydrates	14.7g
Protein	23.2 g
Cholesterol	102 mg
Sodium	231 mg

Ingredients

- 1/4 C. vegetable oil
- 1 C. sliced mushrooms
- 1 C. grated carrot
- 1 C. chopped celery
- 1 C. chopped onion
- 2 cloves garlic, minced
- 1/4 C. chopped fresh parsley
- 2 eggs
- 1/2 C. water
- salt and pepper to taste
- 8 C. cubed white bread
- 5 lb. veal breast
- 1 tsp paprika
- 1/2 tsp onion powder
- 3/4 tsp garlic powder
- salt and pepper to taste

Directions

1. Set your oven to 400 degrees F before doing anything else.
2. In a large skillet, heat the vegetable oil on medium-high heat and cook the mushrooms for about 1-2 minutes.
3. Add the carrot, celery, and onion and cook for about 5-10 minutes.
4. Remove from the heat and stir in the garlic and parsley.
5. In a large bowl, add the eggs, water, salt and pepper and beat well.
6. Fold in the bread cubes till they absorb the egg mixture.
7. Fold in the cooked vegetables and keep aside.
8. With a long, narrow knife, cut a deep pocket into the veal breast.
9. Stuff the veal with the bread and vegetable mixture and sprinkle with the paprika, onion powder, garlic powder, salt and pepper.
10. Arrange the stuffed veal breasts onto a roasting pan and loosely, cover with a piece of foil.
11. Cook in the oven for about 3 1/2 hours.
12. Remove the piece of foil and baste with the pan drippings and cook in the oven for about 30 minutes more.
13. Remove from the oven and tent with the piece of foil for about 15 minutes before slicing.

Homemade Veal Wienerschnitzel

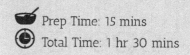

Prep Time: 15 mins
Total Time: 1 hr 30 mins

Servings per Recipe: 4
Calories   515 kcal
Fat   29.1 g
Carbohydrates   33.7g
Protein   29.1 g
Cholesterol   230 mg
Sodium   782 mg

Ingredients

- 1 1/2 lb. veal cutlets
- 1/2 C. all-purpose flour
- 3 tbsp grated Parmesan cheese
- 2 eggs
- 1 tsp minced parsley
- 1/2 tsp salt
- 1/4 tsp pepper
- 1 pinch ground nutmeg
- 2 tbsp milk
- 1 C. dry bread crumbs
- 6 tbsp butter
- 4 slices lemon

Directions

1. Place each veal cutlets between two pieces of plastic wrap and with the flat side of meat mallet, pound into about 1/4 inch thickness.
2. Coat the veal cutlets in flour evenly.
3. In a medium bowl, mix together the Parmesan cheese, eggs, parsley, salt, pepper, nutmeg and milk.
4. In a plate, place the bread crumbs.
5. Dip each cutlet into the egg mixture and then coat in the bread crumbs.
6. Place coated cutlets on a plate and refrigerate for about 1 hour or overnight.
7. In a large skillet, melt the butter on medium heat and cook the cutlets for about 3 minutes per side.
8. Transfer the cutlets into a serving platter and top with the pan juices.
9. Serve with a garnishing of the lemon slices.

VEAL MEATBALL Appetizer

Prep Time: 30 mins
Total Time: 1 hr

Servings per Recipe: 6
Calories 387 kcal
Fat 19.7 g
Carbohydrates 21.1g
Protein 32.4 g
Cholesterol 135 mg
Sodium 2090 mg

Ingredients

6 C. prepared tomato sauce
1/2 C. dry bread crumbs
1/4 C. milk
1 large egg
2 tsp Italian herb seasoning
2 tsp olive oil
1/2 tsp garlic powder
1/4 tsp red pepper flakes
1 lb. ground beef
1 lb. ground veal
1 1/2 tsp salt
1/2 tsp freshly ground black pepper
1/4 tsp ground white pepper (optional)
1/3 C. finely grated Parmigiano-Reggiano cheese

Directions

1. In a large soup pan, add the tomato sauce and bring to a simmer on medium heat.
2. Reduce the heat to low to keep sauce warm while preparing meatballs.
3. Set the broiler of your oven and arrange oven rack about 6-inches from the heating element.
4. Line a baking sheet with a lightly, greased piece of foil.
5. In a bowl, add the bread crumbs, milk, egg, Italian herb seasoning, olive oil, garlic powder and red pepper flakes and beat till a thick slurry forms.
6. In a large bowl, mix together the beef, veal, salt, black pepper and white pepper.
7. Sprinkle with the Parmigiano-Reggiano cheese.
8. Add the slurry and mix till well combined.
9. Make small 48 equal sized balls from the mixture and arrange onto the prepared baking sheet in a single layer.
10. Cook under the broiler for about 4-5 minutes.
11. Flip and cook for about 3-4 minutes more.
12. Transfer meatballs into the simmering tomato sauce and gently stir to combine.
13. Increase the heat to medium and cook for about 5-10 minutes.

Chicken and Veal Roast

Prep Time: 30 mins
Total Time: 6 hr

Servings per Recipe: 12
Calories   111 kcal
Fat   2.6 g
Carbohydrates   2.2g
Protein   < 18.7 g
Cholesterol   49 mg
Sodium   455 mg

Ingredients

- 3 lb. chicken
- 1 veal knuckle
- 2 stalks celery
- 1 yellow onion
- 1 turnip
- 1 carrots
- 2 tsp salt
- 4 quarts water

Directions

1. In a soup pan, mix together the water, veal meat, veal bone, chicken, vegetables and salt and bring to a boil.
2. Reduce the heat and simmer, covered for about 5 hours.
3. Strain the stock and keep aside to cool.
4. Discard the vegetables and bones.

APRIL'S SHOWER
Bacon Soup

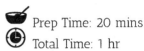
Prep Time: 20 mins
Total Time: 1 hr

Servings per Recipe: 8
Calories   556 kcal
Fat   29.7 g
Carbohydrates   48.1g
Protein   27.1 g
Cholesterol   30 mg
Sodium   1834 mg

Directions

1. Set your oven to 425 degrees F before doing anything else.
2. In a pan, add the beef broth and bring to a boil on medium-high heat.
3. Reduce the heat to medium-low to keep hot.
4. In another large pan, heat 1 tbsp of the olive oil on medium heat and sauté the green onion till tender.
5. Stir in the pancetta and stir fry the pancetta till browned.
6. Increase the heat to medium-high.
7. Stir in the ground veal and cook till crumbly and browned completely.
8. Drain and discard any excess grease.
9. Stir in the artichoke hearts and cook for about 1 minute.
10. Stir in the peas, fava beans, asparagus and 1 1/2 tsp of the salt.
11. Add the hot beef broth and simmer for about 7-10 minutes.
12. Meanwhile in a bowl, add the bread slices, leaves from 7 thyme sprigs, garlic, 1/2 C. olive oil, 1/2 tsp salt and pepper and toss to coat well.
13. Transfer the bread mixture onto a baking sheet.
14. Cook in the oven for about 10 minutes.
15. Stir the leaves of 13 thyme sprigs into the soup and season with the pepper.
16. Divide the hot soup in bowls and top with the croutons and Parmesan cheese.
17. Serve with a drizzling of the extra-virgin olive oil.

Ingredients

- 2 quarts beef broth
- 1 tbsp olive oil
- 2 C. minced green onions
- 5 oz. turkey bacon, minced
- 1/2 lb. ground veal
- 2 C. frozen artichoke hearts, thawed
- 2 C. peas
- 2 C. shelled fava beans
- 2 C. sliced fresh asparagus
- 1 1/2 tsp salt
- 8 slices day-old crusty bread, cut into 1-inch cubes
- 7 sprigs fresh thyme, leaves stripped
- 2 cloves garlic, crushed
- 1/2 C. olive oil
- 1/2 tsp salt
- ground black pepper to taste
- 13 sprigs fresh thyme, leaves stripped
- 1/2 C. grated Parmesan cheese
- 1/4 C. extra-virgin olive oil

Veal Meatballs II

Prep Time: 20 mins
Total Time: 40 mins

Servings per Recipe: 8
Calories	148 kcal
Fat	7.2 g
Carbohydrates	9.8 g
Protein	10.9 g
Cholesterol	68 mg
Sodium	144 mg

Ingredients

- 1/2 C. cranberry juice
- 1/2 C. cranberries
- 3 tbsp maple syrup
- salt and ground black pepper to taste
- 1 lb. lean ground veal
- 1 egg, beaten
- 1 slice bread, crumbled
- 2 tsp chopped fresh rosemary
- 1 C. diced Cheddar cheese

Directions

1. Set your oven to 450 degrees F before doing anything else and line a baking sheet with the parchment paper.
2. Place the prepared baking sheet in the oven.
3. In a skillet, mix together the cranberry juice, cranberries and maple syrup and bring to a boil.
4. Reduce the heat to low and simmer for about 10 minutes.
5. In a blender, add the cranberry mixture in batches and pulse till smooth.
6. Season the pureed cranberry sauce with the salt and pepper.
7. In a bowl, mix together the veal, egg, bread crumbs, rosemary, salt and pepper.
8. Make the balls by pressing the meat mixture around the Cheddar cheese cubes.
9. Arrange the meatballs onto the prepared baking sheet.
10. Cook in the oven for about 8-10 minutes.
11. Serve the meatballs with the cranberry sauce.

MILANESE SPECIALTY
Veal Shanks (Osso Buco)

Prep Time: 20 mins
Total Time: 8 hr 50 mins

Servings per Recipe: 6
Calories	522 kcal
Fat	21 g
Carbohydrates	14.6 g
Protein	64.7 g
Cholesterol	256 mg
Sodium	489 mg

Ingredients

2 tbsp all-purpose flour
salt and pepper to taste
6 (1 inch) thick slices veal shank, sliced for osso buco
2 tbsp butter
2 tbsp olive oil
2 onions, roughly chopped
2 large carrots, chopped
2 stalks celery, chopped
2 cloves garlic, thinly sliced
1 1/4 C. chicken stock
1 (14 oz.) can diced tomatoes
2 tsp chopped fresh oregano
1 bay leaf

Directions

1. In a bowl, mix together the flour, salt and pepper.
2. Add the veal shank slices and toss to coat well.
3. In a large skillet, melt the butter and olive oil on medium heat and cook the shank slices for about 10 minutes per side.
4. In a large slow cooker, mix together the onions, carrots, celery and garlic and top with the shank slices.
5. Place the chicken stock and diced tomatoes and season with the oregano and the bay leaf.
6. Set the slow cooker on Low and cook, covered for about 8 hours.
7. Season with the salt and pepper before serving.

Authentic French Sauce (Demi-Glace)

Prep Time: 30 mins
Total Time: 1 d 5 h 15 mins

Servings per Recipe: 36
Calories   19 kcal
Fat   < 0.5 g
Carbohydrates   < 3.6 g
Protein   0.5 g
Cholesterol   0 mg
Sodium   58 mg

Ingredients

- 10 lb. veal bones (joint and marrow bones)
- 1 tbsp vegetable oil
- 3 onions, cut into eighths
- 4 carrots, cut into 2-inch pieces
- 4 ribs celery, cut into 2-inch pieces
- 1 (6 oz.) can tomato paste
- 10 quarts cold water
- 2 C. cold water

Directions

1. Set your oven to 450 degrees F before doing anything else.
2. In a roasting pan, place the veal bones.
3. Cook in the oven for about 75 minutes.
4. Meanwhile drizzle a baking sheet with the oil.
5. Spread the onion, carrots and celery onto baking sheet and top with the tomato paste evenly.
6. Cook in the oven for about 45 minutes.
7. Transfer the vegetable mixture and bones into a large pan with 10 quarts of the water.
8. Pour 2 C. of the water into the bones roasting pan and place on high heat.
9. Bring to a boil, scraping the browned bits from the bottom of the pan.
10. Place the pan liquid into the pan with the bones.
11. Bring bones, vegetables, and water to a boil.
12. Reduce the heat to low and simmer gently for about 18 hours, skimming foam as necessary.
13. Set a colander over a large bowl and ladle vegetables, bones, and meat into colander.
14. Discard the vegetables, bones and meat and return any broth to the stockpot.

15. Bring broth to a boil and boil for about 30-60 minutes.
16. Strain broth through a fine-mesh strainer into a large container set in an ice bath.
17. Keep aside in room temperature to cool.
18. Cover the container with a lid and refrigerate to chill for about 8 hours to overnight.
19. Scrape and discard any fat from the surface of set demi-glace.
20. Turn demi-glace out onto a work surface. Cut into 16 blocks, wrap each block in plastic wrap, and place wrapped blocks in a resealable plastic bag.
21. Store in the freezer.

Italian Style Veal Shanks

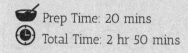

Prep Time: 20 mins
Total Time: 2 hr 50 mins

Servings per Recipe: 7
Calories	251 kcal
Fat	14.5 g
Carbohydrates	10.6 g
Protein	19.7 g
Cholesterol	83 mg
Sodium	947 mg

Ingredients

- 1/4 C. all-purpose flour
- 2 tsp salt
- 1/4 tsp ground black pepper
- 2 lb. veal shank
- 3 tbsp butter
- 3 tbsp olive oil
- 1 C. chopped onion
- 1 C. thinly sliced carrots
- 1/2 C. chopped celery
- 2 cloves garlic, crushed
- 1 (8 oz.) can tomato sauce
- 1 C. water
- 1 tsp dried basil
- 1 tsp dried thyme
- 3 sprigs fresh parsley
- 1 bay leaf

Directions

1. In a shallow dish, mix together the flour, salt and black pepper.
2. Coat the veal shanks with the seasoned flour evenly.
3. In a large skillet, melt the butter and oil on medium heat and sear the shanks till browned completely.
4. Transfer the shanks into a plate and keep aside.
5. In the same skillet, add the onion, carrots, celery and garlic and sauté for about 5 minutes.
6. Stir in the tomato sauce, water, basil, thyme, parsley, bay leaf and shanks and bring to a boil.
7. Reduce the heat to low and simmer, covered for about 2 1/2 hours.

EASIER
Wiener Schnitzel

Prep Time: 20 mins
Total Time: 35 mins

Servings per Recipe: 8	
Calories	435 kcal
Fat	12.4 g
Carbohydrates	51g
Protein	27.4 g
Cholesterol	169 mg
Sodium	479 mg

Ingredients

2 lb. veal
1 C. all-purpose flour
4 eggs
1 tbsp vegetable oil
salt and pepper to taste
4 C. bread crumbs
1/8 C. oil for frying

Directions

1. Cut the veal into steaks, about as thick as your finger.
2. Coat the veal pieces in flour.
3. In a shallow dish, add the eggs, 1 tbsp of the oil, salt and pepper and beat well.
4. Dip the veal in egg mixture and then coat with the bread crumbs.
5. In a heavy skillet, heat 1/4 C. of the oil on medium heat and fry the veal for about 5 minutes per side.

Sunday's Rustic Dinner

Prep Time: 15 mins
Total Time: 1 hr 15 mins

Servings per Recipe: 4
Calories   356 kcal
Fat   24.8 g
Carbohydrates   4.7 g
Protein   29.7 g
Cholesterol   132 mg
Sodium   416 mg

Ingredients

- 1 lb. lean veal chops
- salt and ground black pepper to taste
- 1 pinch ground cumin
- 3 tbsp butter, thinly sliced
- 2 oz. shredded mozzarella cheese
- 2 oz. shredded provolone cheese
- 2 oz. shredded white Cheddar cheese
- 1 (16 oz.) package sliced fresh mushrooms
- 2 tbsp water

Directions

1. Set your oven to 350 degrees F before doing anything else.
2. Season the veal chops with salt, black pepper and cumin evenly.
3. In the bottom of a 13x9-inch casserole dish, place 3-4 butter slices and top with 1/4 of the mozzarella cheese, 1/4 of the provolone cheese and 1/4 of the white Cheddar cheese.
4. Arrange a layer of veal chops over the cheese layer and top each chop with 2-3 butter slices butter, followed by 1/3 of the mushrooms, 1/4 of the mozzarella cheese, 1/4 of the provolone cheese and 1/4 of the white Cheddar cheese.
5. Repeat the layers with the remaining ingredients.
6. Add enough water into the casserole dish to just cover the bottom.
7. Cover the casserole dish with piece of foil and then with an oven-safe lid.
8. Cook in the oven for about 1 hour.

TARRAGON Veal Steaks

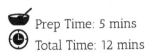

Prep Time: 5 mins
Total Time: 12 mins

Servings per Recipe: 4
Calories   280.7
Fat   15.3g
Cholesterol   149.5mg
Sodium   748.4mg
Carbohydrates   0.4g
Protein   33.1g

Ingredients

4 (6 oz.) boneless veal steaks
1 tsp salt
1/2 tsp pepper
4 tsp butter
1 tsp parsley
1 tsp tarragon
1 tsp chives

Directions

1. Pound the steaks into 1/8-inch thickness.
2. Sprinkle the steaks with the salt and pepper.
3. In a large skillet, melt the butter on medium-high heat and cook the steaks for about 3 minutes per side.
4. Add remaining ingredients and cook for about 1 minute more.

Bavarian Style Veal

Prep Time: 10 mins
Total Time: 25 mins

Servings per Recipe: 4
Calories   637.4
Fat   49.8g
Cholesterol   161.0mg
Sodium   283.1mg
Carbohydrates   9.0g
Protein   33.9g

Ingredients

- 1/2 lb veal, cut into strips
- 1/2 lb chicken, cut into strips
- 3 C. sliced mushrooms
- 3 tbsp oil
- salt and pepper
- 2 tbsp butter
- 2 tbsp chopped shallots
- 1/2 C. broth
- 1/2 C. chicken broth
- 1 tbsp chives
- 1 tbsp parsley
- 1 tbsp tarragon
- 2 C. sour cream

Directions

1. In a skillet, heat the oil and sear the veal and chicken till browned and done.
2. Transfer the meat mixture in a bowl.
3. In the same skillet, sauté the mushrooms till browned.
4. Transfer the mushrooms in the bowl with the meat mixture.
5. In another skillet, melt the butter in skillet and sauté the shallots till tender.
6. Add the broth and cook till almost all the liquid is absorbed.
7. Add the chicken broth and meat drippings and cook till reduces by 1/3.
8. Stir in the spices and sour cream.
9. Add meat and mushrooms mixture and cook till heated through.
10. Serve with the noodles.

MILANESE
Veal Scaloppini

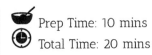
Prep Time: 10 mins
Total Time: 20 mins

Servings per Recipe: 4
Calories	218.6
Fat	21.2g
Cholesterol	136.2mg
Sodium	309.4mg
Carbohydrates	6.2g
Protein	5.1g

Ingredients

2 tbsp olive oil
2 tbsp butter
8 veal scaloppini
flour, mixed with
salt & pepper (for dredging)
2 eggs, and
2 tbsp water, whisked
1 C. chicken broth
1 lemon, juiced
1 lemon, sliced for garnish
fresh parsley (to garnish)
2 tbsp butter

Directions

1. Set your oven to 200 degrees F before doing anything else.
2. In a bowl, mix together the flour, salt and pepper.
3. Coat the veal in flour mixture evenly.
4. In a large skillet, heat oil and butter and cook 4 scallops for about 2 minutes per side.
5. Transfer the scallops into an oven proof plate and place in preheated oven to keep warm.
6. Repeat with 4 scallops.
7. Meanwhile in the same skillet, add the broth and cook till reduces by half.
8. Squeeze the juice of 1 lemon into broth and cook for about 5 minutes.
9. Slowly, add the butter, beating continuously till the sauce thickens.
10. Return the veal and toss to coat.
11. Serve with a garnishing of the lemon slices and parsley.

Tarragon Mushroom Entrée

Prep Time: 10 mins
Total Time: 30 mins

Servings per Recipe: 2
Calories   183.9
Fat   13.9g
Cholesterol   0.9mg
Sodium   46.8mg
Carbohydrates   3.7g
Protein   1.0g

Ingredients

4 veal chops
2 tbsp olive oil
salt and pepper
1 tbsp tarragon
1 lb cremini mushroom, sliced
2 tbsp flour
1 C. chicken stock
2 tbsp heavy cream
1 dash nutmeg

Directions

1. Season the chops with the salt and black pepper.
2. In a skillet, heat the oil and cook the chops for about 5 minutes per side.
3. Transfer the chops into plate and keep warm.
4. In a bowl, add the mushrooms and flour and toss to coat.
5. In the same skillet, add the mushrooms and chicken stock and cook till thickened.
6. Stir in the cream, nutmeg, salt and pepper.
7. Place the sauce over chops and serve.

CHOPS 101

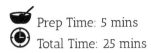
Prep Time: 5 mins
Total Time: 25 mins

Servings per Recipe: 6
Calories	67.8
Fat	6.9g
Cholesterol	0.0mg
Sodium	582.8mg
Carbohydrates	1.5g
Protein	0.3g

Ingredients

1 1/2 tsp salt
1 1/2 tsp garlic powder
1 1/4 tsp onion powder
1 tsp dried thyme leaves
1/2 tsp ground cumin
3/4 tsp dry mustard
1/2 tsp paprika
1/2 tsp black pepper
1/2 tsp white pepper
1/4 tsp cayenne
6 veal chops
3 tbsp olive oil

Directions

1. In a bowl, mix together all the ingredients except the chops and oil.
2. Sprinkle the chops with the seasoning mixture evenly.
3. In a skillet, heat 1 tbsp of the olive oil and cook the chops in batches for about 3 minutes.
4. Flip the side and cook for about 2-3 minutes.
5. Transfer the chops into a bowl.
6. Repeat with the remaining olive oil and remaining chops.

Backroad Wandering Veal Stew

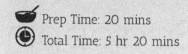

Prep Time: 20 mins
Total Time: 5 hr 20 mins

Servings per Recipe: 8
Calories 67.8
Fat 6.9g
Cholesterol 0.0mg
Sodium 582.8mg
Carbohydrates 1.5g
Protein 0.3g

Ingredients

2 1/2 lbs stewing veal, trimmed and cubed
1/3 C. flour
2 tbsp vegetable oil
2 tbsp butter
1 onion, chopped
3 leeks, chopped (white and light green parts only!)
2 garlic cloves, minced
1 bay leaf
3/4 tsp salt
3/4 tsp pepper
1/4 tsp ground nutmeg
2 1/2 C. chicken stock
4 C. small button mushrooms
2 C. shiitake mushroom caps
2 tbsp lemon juice
1/2 C. whipping cream
1/4 C. fresh parsley, chopped

Directions

1. In a large plastic bag, add the veal and flour and shake to coat.
2. In a large shallow Dutch oven, heat the oil on medium-high heat and cook the veal in batches till browned.
3. Transfer the veal into slow cooker.
4. Drain the fat from Dutch oven and melt 1 tbsp of the butter on medium heat.
5. Add the onions, leeks, garlic and lay leaf and sauté for about 5 minutes.
6. Add 1/2 tsp each of the salt and pepper, all the thyme, nutmeg and stock and bring to a boil, scraping up any brown bits from the bottom of the pan.
7. Place the stock mixture over the veal in slow cooker.
8. Set the slow cooker on High and cook, covered for about 4-5 hours.
9. In a large skillet, melt the remaining butter on medium-high heat and sauté the mushrooms, remaining salt and pepper for about 10 minutes.
10. Add the mushroom mixture into slow cooker with the lemon juice and cook, covered on High for about 15 minutes.
11. Discard the bay leaf and stir in the cream and parsley.

HOMEMADE Scaloppini

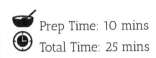

Prep Time: 10 mins
Total Time: 25 mins

Servings per Recipe: 4
Calories   61.2
Fat   3.8g
Cholesterol   0.0mg
Sodium   298.4mg
Carbohydrates   8.7g
Protein   1.4g

Ingredients

extra virgin olive oil, as needed
1 tsp minced garlic
2 C. chopped tomatoes
salt and pepper
1 C. mixed good olive
8 -12 slices veal, thin slices, preferably from the leg, pounded slightly until less than 1/4 inch thick
flour, for dredging
1 lemon, thinly sliced
chopped fresh parsley leaves (to garnish)

Directions

1. Set your oven to 200 degrees F before doing anything else.
2. In a medium pan, heat 2 tbsp of the olive oil on medium heat and sauté the garlic till sizzles.
3. Add the tomatoes, salt and pepper and cook about 10 minutes, stirring occasionally.
4. Stir in the olives and reduce the heat to low.
5. Sprinkle the veal with salt and pepper and then coat with the flour.
6. In a large nonstick skillet, heat 3 tbsp of the olive oil on medium-high heat and sear the veal slices in batches for about 5 minutes per side.
7. Transfer the slices into a plate and keep warm in oven while searing the remaining slices.
8. Pour the sauce over the veal slices and arrange lemon on top.
9. Serve with a sprinkling of the parsley.

Veal Fontina

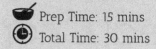
Prep Time: 15 mins
Total Time: 30 mins

Servings per Recipe: 2	
Calories	830.8
Fat	60.9g
Cholesterol	243.0mg
Sodium	117.7mg
Carbohydrates	26.3g
Protein	28.7g

Ingredients

- 9 oz. veal, scallops
- 1 tsp dried sage, crumbled
- fresh ground pepper
- 6 pieces turkey bacon
- 6 pieces Fontina cheese, sliced thin
- 1/2 C. all-purpose flour
- 3 tbsp unsalted butter
- 3/4 C. broth
- 6 tbsp chilled unsalted butter, cut into pieces
- salt
- lemon wedge

Directions

1. Place 1 veal scallop between sheets of waxed paper and with a rolling pin, flatten to 1/8-inch thickness.
2. Repeat with the remaining veal scallops.
3. Season veal scallops with the sage and pepper.
4. Coat the veal in flour and shake off the excess.
5. In heavy large skillet, melt 3 tbsp of the butter on medium heat and cook the veal scallops for about 2-3 minutes per side.
6. Place a slice of bacon and fontina over each veal slice.
7. Cover the pan briefly and cook till the prosciutto the fontina is melted completely.
8. Transfer the veal scallops into platter and tent with the foil to keep warm.
9. Discard the fat from skillet.
10. In the same skillet, add broth and bring to a boil, scraping up any browned bits and cook for about 8 minutes.
11. Reduce the heat to low.
12. Add the chilled butter, 1 tbsp at a time, beating continuously.
13. Season with the salt and pepper.
14. Place the sauce over veal and serve with a garnishing of the lemon wedges.

SICILIAN STYLE
Veal Chops

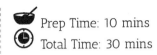
Prep Time: 10 mins
Total Time: 30 mins

Servings per Recipe: 2
Calories	205.7
Fat	13.2g
Cholesterol	10.0mg
Sodium	462.6mg
Carbohydrates	17.0g
Protein	2.2g

Ingredients

- 2 veal loin chops
- 1 large shallot
- 2 cloves garlic
- 1/2 tsp crushed red pepper flakes
- 2 tsp chopped fresh parsley
- 4 tsp extra virgin olive oil
- 2 tsp butter
- 1/4 C. broth
- 1 (14 oz.) cans diced tomatoes (preferably with garlic and basil)
- 2 tsp dried thyme, crushed to a course powder
- salt and pepper

Directions

1. Sprinkle the chops with the thyme, salt and pepper.
2. In a heavy skillet, heat 2 tbsp of the oil on medium-high heat and cook the chops till browned from both sides.
3. Transfer the chops into a plate.
4. In the same skillet, heat 1 tbsp of the oil and sauté the shallots, garlic and crushed red pepper till tender.
5. Add the broth and bring to a boil and cook till reduces by half.
6. Add the tomatoes and their juices and bring to a boil.
7. Add the chops and reduce the heat to medium.
8. Cook, covered for about 10 minutes.
9. Transfer the chops into a serving platter.
10. In the same skillet, add the butter and half of the parsley and swirl till the butter just melts and the sauce starts to thicken.
11. Spoon the sauce over the chops and drizzle with the remaining 1 tbsp of the olive oil.
12. Serve with a sprinkling of the remaining parsley.

Veal Escape

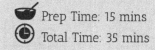
Prep Time: 15 mins
Total Time: 35 mins

Servings per Recipe: 2
Calories   183.9
Fat   13.9g
Cholesterol   0.9mg
Sodium   46.8mg
Carbohydrates   3.7g
Protein   1.0g

Ingredients

2 veal chops (about 3/4-inch thick)
2 cloves garlic, finely chopped
1 tbsp fresh rosemary, finely chopped
2 tbsp olive oil
salt & freshly ground black pepper
1/2 C. broth
1/4 C. chicken stock

Directions

1. Set your oven to 375 degrees F before doing anything else.
2. Rub the veal chops with 1 tbsp of the oil, garlic, rosemary, salt and pepper and keep aside for about 15 minutes.
3. In a large cast iron skillet, heat the remaining oil on medium-high heat and cook the chops to pan and cook till golden brown from one side.
4. Transfer the chops into a baking dish, brown side down.
5. Cook in the oven for about 10 minutes.
6. Add broth and stock to cast iron pan and scrape the brown bits from the bottom.
7. Serve chops with the pan juices.

25-MINUTE Veal Meal

Prep Time: 15 mins
Total Time: 25 mins

Servings per Recipe: 4
Calories   917.4
Fat   42.4g
Cholesterol   233.7mg
Sodium   414.9mg
Carbohydrates   106.5g
Protein   26.1g

Ingredients

4 veal cutlets
4 oz. butter
1/4 C. olive oil
2 oz. Brie cheese
2 oz. flour
2 oz. breadcrumbs
3 eggs

1 lb fresh pasta
grated Parmesan cheese
salt & freshly ground black pepper

Directions

1. In a shallow bowl, add the egg, a little oil, salt and pepper and beat.
2. In a second shallow bowl, place the flour.
3. In a third shallow bowl, place the bread crumbs.
4. With meat mallet, flatten the veal cutlets by placing between 2 plastic wrap sheets.
5. Place Brie slices over the veal cutlets and fold in two.
6. Coat the veal cutlets in the flour evenly.
7. Dip in egg mixture and then coat in bread crumbs.
8. In a skillet, heat the oil and butter and cook the cutlets for about 5 minutes per side.
9. In a serving plate, place the cutlets with fresh pasta and a slice of lemon.
10. Serve with a topping of the grated Parmesan.

Panhandle Cuisine Stew

Prep Time: 10 mins
Total Time: 1 hr 5 mins

Servings per Recipe: 4
Calories   241.0
Fat   15.3g
Cholesterol   78.1mg
Sodium   1391.1mg
Carbohydrates   12.5g
Protein   13.3g

Ingredients

1/2 lb veal, for braising
1/2 C. ground veal (shape into little meatballs)
2 C. water
1 tsp salt
1 onion
1 large carrot
1/2 C. fresh parsley
1/2 tsp thyme
1 bay leaf
1 pinch mace
6 peppercorns
SAUCE
2 C. broth, from braising the veal
3 tbsp butter
4 tbsp flour
1 tbsp lemon juice
2 tbsp cream

Directions

1. For broth in a pan, melt some butter and cook the veal pieces till browned completely.
2. Add the water, salt, whole vegetables, herbs and seasonings and cook for about 45 minutes.
3. Add the meatballs and simmer for about 10 minutes.
4. With a slotted spoon, transfer the solids into a large bowl.
5. Discard the vegetables, herbs and seasonings.
6. Slice the veal into small bite size pieces.
7. For sauce, in another pan, melt the butter and cook the flour for a few minutes, stirring continuously.
8. Slowly, add the broth, stirring continuously.
9. Add meatballs, veal pieces, lemon, juice and cream and stir to combine.
10. Serve over the rice, pasta or mashed potatoes.

FREE CITY
Veal

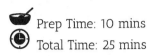
Prep Time: 10 mins
Total Time: 25 mins

Servings per Recipe: 4
Calories   241.0
Fat   15.3g
Cholesterol   78.1mg
Sodium   1391.1mg
Carbohydrates   12.5g
Protein   13.3g

Ingredients

3 tbsp butter
8 veal scallops, floured and seasoned
1 1/2 C. heavy cream, heated
1 lemon, juice of
fresh parsley, chopped
1 dash paprika
salt and pepper

Directions

1. Set your oven to 250 degrees F before doing anything else.
2. In nonstick frying pan, melt half of the butter on high heat and sear half of the veal scallops for about 2 minutes per side.
3. Transfer the veal scallops in a baking dish.
4. Repeat with the remaining veal scallops and keep hot in the oven.
5. In the same frying pan, add the lemon juice and cook for about 1 minute on high heat.
6. Stir in the cream and parsley and cook for about 3-4 minutes.
7. Return the veal scallops in the frying pan and sprinkle with the paprika.
8. Cook for about 1 minute.

Simply Breaded Veal

Prep Time: 1 hr
Total Time: 1 hr 5 mins

Servings per Recipe: 4
Calories   81.8
Fat   2.6g
Cholesterol   55.3mg
Sodium   73.8mg
Carbohydrates   10.9g
Protein   3.2g

Ingredients

4 veal cutlets
1/4 C. flour
1/4 C. breadcrumbs, seasoned
1 egg, beaten
1 tsp garlic oil
1 tsp butter

Directions

1. With a meat mallet, pound the veal cutlets into 1/4-inch thickness.
2. Coat the cutlets in flour evenly.
3. Dip in the egg and coat with the bread crumbs.
4. Cover with the wax paper and refrigerate for at least 1 hour.
5. In a skillet, heat the oil and butter and cook the cutlets for about 2 minutes per side.

VEAL
Parmigiana

Prep Time: 15 mins
Total Time: 1 hr 3 mins

Servings per Recipe: 4
Calories   81.8
Fat   2.6g
Cholesterol   55.3mg
Sodium   73.8mg
Carbohydrates   10.9g
Protein   3.2g

Ingredients

- 4 veal cutlets
- 2 beaten eggs
- 2 C. breadcrumbs
- 2 tbsp olive oil
- 1 tsp salt
- 1 tsp pepper
- 1 tbsp parsley
- 1 tbsp garlic powder
- 1/4 C. Parmesan cheese
- 1 C. tomato sauce

Directions

1. Set your oven to 350 degrees F before doing anything else.
2. In a bowl add 2 eggs and beat.
3. In another bowl, mix together the bread crumbs, salt, pepper, garlic and parsley.
4. Dip the veal in eggs then coat in bread crumb mixture.
5. In an oven proof skillet, heat the oil and cook the veal for about 3 minutes per side.
6. Top the veal with the tomato sauce and sprinkle with the Parmesan cheese.
7. Cook in the oven for about 30-45 minutes.

Artisanal Veal

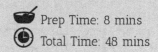
Prep Time: 8 mins
Total Time: 48 mins

Servings per Recipe: 4
Calories   345.9
Fat   15.9g
Cholesterol   140.5mg
Sodium   215.0mg
Carbohydrates   15.1g
Protein   35.8g

Ingredients

- 4 (6 oz.) lean veal chops (3/4 inch thick), trimmed
- 1 tsp cracked black pepper
- cooking spray
- 1/3 C. sliced green pepper
- 3/4 C. sliced sweet pepper, orange, red and yellow
- 1/3 C. reduced-fat-free chicken broth
- 1/4 tsp dried whole thyme
- 2 garlic cloves, minced
- 1 (14 oz.) cans artichoke hearts, drained and quartered
- 2 tbsp chopped fresh parsley

Directions

1. Set your oven to 350 degrees F before doing anything else.
2. Rub the cracked pepper over chops evenly.
3. Grease a large oven proof nonstick skillet with cooking spray and heat on medium-high heat.
4. Add the chops and cook for about 3-4 minutes per side.
5. Transfer the chops into a bowl and keep aside.
6. With a paper towel, wipe the drippings from skillet.
7. In the same skillet, add the green pepper, sweet pepper, chicken broth, thyme and garlic and bring to a boil.
8. Reduce the heat and simmer for about 5 minutes.
9. Stir in the artichoke hearts and chops.
10. Cover and cook in the oven for about 25 minutes.
11. Serve immediately with a sprinkling of the chopped parsley.

HOW TO MAKE
Rump Roast

🥣 Prep Time: 30 mins
🕐 Total Time: 2 hr 30 mins

Servings per Recipe: 4
Calories 718.6
Fat 15.9g
Cholesterol 140.5mg
Sodium 215.0mg
Carbohydrates 15.1g
Protein 35.8g

Ingredients

3 lbs boneless veal rump roast, tied
2 tbsp flour
1/2 tsp sea salt
1/4 tsp fresh ground black pepper
2 tbsp olive oil
1 tsp paprika
1/3 C. shallot, minced
1 C. broth
1 1/4 C. chicken stock

1/2 tsp dried rosemary
1/2 tsp dried thyme
2 tbsp butter
2 tbsp brown sugar, packed
10 oz. white pearl onions, peeled
1 lb baby carrots
3 small turnips, peeled and wedged
2 large parsnips, 1" pieces

Directions

1. Set your oven to 325 degrees F before doing anything else.
2. Coat the veal with the flour evenly and season with the salt and pepper.
3. In a large pan, heat the olive oil on medium-high heat and sear the veal till browned from all sides.
4. Transfer the veal into a roasting pan and sprinkle with the paprika.
5. In the same pan, add the shallots and cook for about 3 minutes.
6. Stir in the broth and 3/4 C. of the chicken stock and bring to a boil.
7. Place the broth mixture over the veal and sprinkle with the rosemary and thyme.
8. Bring veal roast to a simmer over medium heat.
9. Cover the roasting pan and cook in the oven for about 1 1/4 hours.
10. In a frying pan, melt the butter and sugar and stir in the onions, carrots, turnips and parsnips till coated completely.
11. Add the salt, pepper and remaining 1/2 C. of the chicken stock and bring to a roaring boil.
12. Reduce the heat and simmer, uncovered for about 10 minutes, stirring occasionally.
13. Remove the roasting pan from the oven and arrange the vegetables around the veal and

baste the vegetables with the pan juices.
14. Cover roast and cook in the oven for about 30-45 minutes.
15. Remove from the oven and place the veal in a plate, covered with a tin foil for about 10 minutes.
16. Transfer the vegetables into a serving platter.
17. Place the roasting pan on stove and cook till the sauce reduces.
18. Slice the veal and place into the platter with vegetables.
19. Serve with a drizzling of the sauce.

BAKED
Veal Cutlets

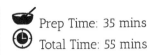
Prep Time: 35 mins
Total Time: 55 mins

Servings per Recipe: 6
Calories   544.8
Fat   35.1g
Cholesterol   186.2mg
Sodium   664.1mg
Carbohydrates   22.5g
Protein   36.0g

Ingredients

1/2 C. vegetable oil, divided
1 small onion, chopped
1 garlic clove, crushed
3 (15 oz.) cans chopped tomatoes, undrained
1 (6 oz.) cans tomato paste
1 tsp chopped fresh basil
1/2 tsp dried oregano
1 bay leaf
24 oz. veal cutlets
2 eggs, beaten
1/2 C. breadcrumbs, seasoned
1 C. mozzarella cheese, shredded
1/2 C. Parmesan cheese, grated and divided

Directions

1. Set your oven to 400 degrees F before doing anything else and grease a large casserole dish.
2. Pound the veal to 1/4-inch thickness.
3. In a large skillet, heat 2 tbsp of the oil on medium-high heat and sauté the onion and garlic for about 5 minutes.
4. Stir in the tomatoes, tomato paste, basil, oregano and bay leaf and simmer for about 20 minutes, stirring occasionally.
5. Discard the bay leaf.
6. Dip veal cutlets into egg and coat with the breadcrumbs.
7. In another skillet, heat the remaining oil and sear the veal cutlets for about 5 minutes per side.
8. Drain the grease from the pan.
9. In the prepared casserole dish, place the tomato mixture, followed by the veal cutlets, mozzarella, 1/4 C. of the Parmesan.
10. Cook in the oven for about 15 minutes.
11. Serve with a sprinkling of the remaining Parmesan.

Northern Italy Style Veal Shanks (Osso Buco III)

Prep Time: 20 mins
Total Time: 2 hr

Servings per Recipe: 4
Calories 175.1
Fat 14.9g
Cholesterol 2.5mg
Sodium 198.6mg
Carbohydrates 6.1g
Protein 2.1g

Ingredients

4 veal shanks (cut 2-inch thick)
2 tbsp flour
salt & freshly ground black pepper, to taste
1/4 C. olive oil
1 tsp butter
1 C. chopped tomato
1 C. chicken broth
1/4 C. broth
2 tbsp fresh lemon juice
2 - 4 fresh basil leaves, chopped 1
1 spring fresh rosemary (optional)
1 dash cinnamon
1/2 tsp garlic powder
2 - 4 carrots, peeled (optional)

Directions

1. Set your oven to 375 degrees F before doing anything else.
2. Season the shanks with the salt and pepper and dust with the flour.
3. In a large skillet, heat the olive oil and butter and sear the shanks till browned completely.
4. Transfer the shanks into a large baking dish.
5. Arrange the carrots around the shanks.
6. In the same skillet, add the tomatoes, broth, broth, lemon juice, basil, cinnamon and garlic powder and scrap up any browned bits on the bottom of the pan.
7. Place the broth mixture over the shanks.
8. Cover the veal shank with a piece of foil.
9. Cook in the oven for about 1 1/2 hours.

JANUARY NIGHT
Veal Stew

Prep Time: 20 mins
Total Time: 8 hr 20 mins

Servings per Recipe: 8
Calories	283.7
Fat	12.5g
Cholesterol	126.4mg
Sodium	123.2mg
Carbohydrates	8.7g
Protein	28.5g

Ingredients

1 leek, thinly sliced (white and pale green parts only)
3 garlic cloves, pressed
1 tbsp dried tarragon
1/2 tsp lemon zest
1/2 tsp dried thyme
1/2 tsp white pepper
1/4 tsp dried sage
2 1/2-3 lbs veal, trimmed of fat, cubed
1/3 C. all-purpose flour
3/4 C. broth
1/4 C. lemon juice
1 tbsp cornstarch
1/4 C. whipping cream
salt

Directions

1. In a larger slow cooker, mix together the leek, garlic, tarragon, lemon zest, thyme, white pepper and sage.
2. Coat veal cubes with the flour and place in the slow cooker.
3. Add the broth and lemon juice.
4. Set the slow cooker on Low and cook, covered for about 7-8 hours.
5. In a small bowl, mix together the cornstarch and cream.
6. Add the cream mixture into stew and stir to combine well.
7. Now, set the slow cooker on High and cook, covered for about 15 minutes, stirring 2-3 times.
8. Season with the salt.
9. Serve with a garnishing of the fresh tarragon and lemon slices.

Lover's Veal

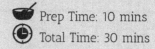

Prep Time: 10 mins
Total Time: 30 mins

Servings per Recipe: 8
Calories	283.7
Fat	12.5g
Cholesterol	126.4mg
Sodium	123.2mg
Carbohydrates	8.7g
Protein	28.5g

Ingredients

- 1 medium eggplant
- 1/4 C. oil, divided, plus additional as needed
- 4 boneless veal steaks
- plain flour
- Italian spices
- 20 g butter
- 1 onion, chopped
- 1 - 2 C. pizza sauce
- 4 oz. mushrooms, drained
- 1 C. black olives, sliced
- 8 slices turkey bacon
- 1 C. mozzarella cheese, grated

Directions

1. Cut the eggplant into 1cm slices.
2. In a large pan, heat a few tbsp of the oil at a time and cook the eggplant slices in batches till well-browned from both sides.
3. Transfer the eggplant slices onto paper towel lined plate.
4. Set the broiler of your oven.
5. Coat the veal in flour and Italian seasonings, shaking off the excess.
6. In a large frying pan, melt the butter and sear the veal till browned from both sides and cooked completely.
7. Transfer the veal into platter and keep warm.
8. In the same pan, heat 1 tbsp of the olive oil and sauté the onion till tender.
9. Add the pizza sauce, mushrooms and olives and simmer till warm.
10. Spread the pizza sauce mixture on broiler-safe platter.
11. Place veal over the pizza sauce, followed by the eggplant, bacon and cheese.
12. Cook under the broiler till the cheese is browned and melted.

CREPES
and Veal

Prep Time: 45 mins
Total Time: 1 hr 15 mins

Servings per Recipe: 8
Calories	557 kcal
Fat	30.1 g
Carbohydrates	39.3g
Protein	32.5 g
Cholesterol	145 mg
Sodium	1423 mg

Ingredients

2 eggs
2/3 C. milk
1 tbsp butter, melted
1/2 C. all-purpose flour
1/4 tsp salt
1/4 pound ground veal
1/4 pound ground chicken
1/2 pound ground beef
2 tbsps butter
1 tbsp minced fresh parsley
1/2 C. grated Parmesan cheese
1/2 tsp salt
1 dash ground black pepper
1 dash ground nutmeg
2 tbsps butter
2 tbsps all-purpose flour
1 C. milk
1/4 tsp salt
1/8 tsp ground black pepper
1/8 tsp ground nutmeg
1 (32 ounce) jar tomato pasta sauce
1 (16 ounce) package shredded mozzarella cheese
1/4 C. grated Parmesan cheese

Directions

1. For the crepes, in a medium bowl, crack the eggs and beat well, then mix in the butter and milk.
2. Add the flour and salt and beat till well combined. (For a better result, keep the mixture aside for at least 30 minutes before cooking)
3. In a lightly, greased skillet, cook the crepes till golden brown in about 6-8 inches size.
4. Set your oven to 375 degrees F.
5. For the filling, in a skillet, melt the butter on medium-high heat.
6. Add the meat and cook till browned completely.
7. Stir in the Parmesan and parsley and remove from heat and keep aside to cool.
8. For the sauce, in a pan, mix together the butter and flour on medium heat and cook, stirring continuously for about 5 minutes.
9. Stir in the nutmeg, salt and pepper, then slowly, add the milk and cook, stirring continuously till the desired thickness.
10. In the bottom of a 13x9-inch baking dish, spread the half of the pasta sauce evenly.
11. Divide the meat mixture in each crepe evenly and fold the all sides to form a roll.
12. Place the crepe rolls over the pasta sauce, seam side down.
13. Place the remaining pasta sauce over the rolls evenly, followed by the white sauce, mozzarella and Parmesan.
14. Cook in the oven for about 20-30 minutes.

Mushrooms and Sour Cream Stew

Prep Time: 20 mins
Total Time: 1 hr 20 mins

Servings per Recipe: 4
Calories   558.5
Fat   19.3g
Cholesterol   242.8mg
Sodium   1034.3mg
Carbohydrates   4.4g
Protein   47.0g

Ingredients

- 3 slices turkey bacon, diced
- 3 tbsps butter
- 1/2 C. sliced mushrooms
- 1/2 C. diced onion
- 2 lbs veal, cut in cubes
- 1/2 C. chicken broth
- 1 C. sour cream
- 1 tsp salt
- 1/2 tsp black pepper
- 1 tsp paprika

Directions

1. Set your oven to 250 degrees before doing anything else.
2. Begin to stir fry the following in butter: mushroom, bacon, and onions. Fry the mix until the bacon is done.
3. Now place the mix in a casserole dish and then begin to brown your veal in the bacon drippings.
4. Once the veal is browned all over place it in the casserole dish as well.
5. Pour in the broth to the pan and also add in: sour cream, salt, paprika, and pepper.
6. Get the mix boiling then add it to the casserole dish as well.
7. Place a covering of foil over everything and cook it all in the oven for 65 mins.
8. Enjoy.

ENJOY THE RECIPES?
KEEP ON COOKING WITH 6 MORE FREE COOKBOOKS!

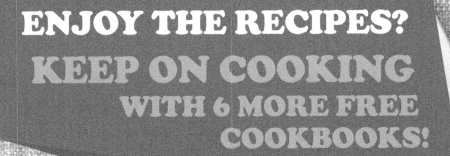

Click the link below and simply enter your email address to join the club and receive your 6 cookbooks.

http://booksumo.com/magnet

https://www.instagram.com/booksumopress/

https://www.facebook.com/booksumo/